Francis Alexander Homfray

Idyls of Thought and Lyrical Pieces

Francis Alexander Homfray

Idyls of Thought and Lyrical Pieces

ISBN/EAN: 9783744770842

Printed in Europe, USA, Canada, Australia, Japan

Cover: Foto ©Thomas Meinert / pixelio.de

More available books at **www.hansebooks.com**

IDYLS OF THOUGHT
AND LYRICAL PIECES

IDYLS OF THOUGHT

AND LYRICAL PIECES

BY

F. A. HOMFRAY
(Franc Alexa.)

LONDON
GEORGE ALLEN, 156, CHARING CROSS ROAD
1898
[*All rights reserved*]

Printed by BALLANTYNE, HANSON & Co.
At the Ballantyne Press

CONTENTS

IDYLS OF THOUGHT—

    IDYL I 3
    IDYL II 8
    IDYL III—
        BUTTERCUP TIME 14
    IDYL IV 21
    IDYL V—
        THE SNOWCLOUDS 28
    IDYL VI—
        A MYSTERY OF MORNING 35
    IDYL VII—
        SHORE THOUGHTS 39

LYRICAL PIECES—

    ROSE BIRTH 51
    THE ELM 53
    THE SCOTCH FIR 55
    ARBOR PONTICA 57

CONTENTS

LYRICAL PIECES (*continued*)—

	PAGE
A Character	59
A Potent Memory	61
Rough Winds at Night	63
A Garden	66
A City Sigh	68
By a Grave	70
Distance	71
At an Open Window	75
Waving Grass	76
The Turning from the Grave	79
A Sprin Fancy	85
'Four Zones in Yonder Evening Sky'	87

IDYLS OF THOUGHT

A

IDYLS OF THOUGHT

IDYL I

I STOOD at eve upon a windswept ridge,
That from the dying landscape turned away
Its meadow-mantled shoulder, and before,
Across a little crooked upland vale
Rich with dim elms and darkening hedgerow
    lines,
Saw the steep rampart of the summit climb
Up to the growing night. The monstrous wall
Reared a grim edge against the windy sky,
Unbroken, save that on the midmost height
Nested aloft, a shadowy hamlet hung ;
And o'er it rose a solitary tower,
Tall, queenlike, ghostlike. All about its crown
Of fretted balustrades and pinnacles
The random shreds and strands of shattered
    cloud,

Torn by the wind, ran riot ; and the gale,
Up from the westward sweeping like a host,
Hurled at the church its gusty myrmidons
In one gray tumult gathering ; while behind
Loomed the sad lights of half-extinguished eve,
Slow-dying, vapour-blinded. As I watched,
With sudden clamour in the pausing wind
I heard the prisoned voices of the tower
Fling out a deep-tongued sequence on the night,
Voice after voice. The strong wind took the sound,
And whirled it up with fragments of the clouds,
Fringes of storm and slanted spears of rain,
Against the airy dome. But still I heard,
Loud in the lull and fainter through the roar,
The dizzy-balanced brazen-throated choir
Stroke after stroke out-swinging. Not the chimes,
The sweet-toned chronicle of hours outworn
For ever ; not the holy vesper-bell,
Or plaintive curfew ; not the jubilant peal,
Sequel of snowy veil and marriage-flowers ;

No, nor the slow heart-sinking knell of death,
That ever seems to cease, yet ceases not,
So long the sad strokes tarry. But the bells
Rang out a tune of ancient psalmody,
Broad, simple, grand ; well-worn by worshippers
On many a Sabbath ; such as village folk
Use, heedless whence the music came, and count
As much an heirloom as the village well.
Yet somewhere, far away perchance, he lies,
In whose full heart of old to God upturned,
Rose like a tide the music of the psalm ;
And even while they sing, the self-same stars
That watch the gray roof of their church, look down
With glistening on the grasses of his grave,
Forgotten. Not, this night, the voice of men
Gave utterance to his holy psalmody,
But the loud company of brazen tongues
Took up, and told it to the stormy winds.
And as the music wandered up the clouds
Thro' rainy tumult, ghostlier seemed the tower,
As if it lived and sang ; and rooted fast
On the high boundary of earth and sky,

Fronting the abyss, and fixed above the hills,
Made, by the potency of sacred sound,
In name of heavenward-turned humanity,
A steadfast answer to the shocks and stress
And stormy roughness of the outer world.
An old abode of worship, vision-like,
Wrought by dead hands, unperishing it stood,
A fortress of the faith of other times,
And speaking with the voice of other days,
The chant of forefathers devout, alive
In children's mouths; both lasting as the need
That gave them being. For the life of man,
Even in the lonely hamlets of the hills,
Still battling against outward circumstance,
Has need to stretch a hand beyond the world
And grasp a higher ; gathering inward strength
And purpose from without. Of this the bells
Bare record, sounding out the solemn psalm,
Above the valley elms, and fields of toil.

 The dark fell deeper on the upward slopes,
And louder swept the gale ; yet still I saw
Even as a dim tall spectre, brazen-voiced,
The great tower singing to the stormy night.

So strong the notes against the vault of heaven
Poured from the grim uplifted battlements,
With such endurance in the windy stress,
It seemed a conscious power, not desolate
In empty clamour, but as if there rose
An answering music somewhere in the spheres.

IDYL II

THE early-dying sad November day
Left yet more colourless the barren down,
And paler every wraith of summer grass
That lingered bloom-bereft; and the gaunt trees,
That all day long had borne the whistling east,
With still more vain beseeching upward stretched
Their line of naked boughs that fringed the plain,
And met a joyless heaven; for overhead
The moody west was dark with gathered cloud.
Yet, as the interminable sandy waste
Bears the green islet for despairing eyes,
While I beheld the blank and weary sky,
There came a shining rift within the cloud,
That widened somewhat, like an open door,
Then grew not larger. But my fancy woke
Amid the dulness of the earth. Yon door,
I thought, whose edges from the rounding dark

Melt inwards into feathery flakes and films
Of vapour dyed with light, hath opening,
If one could mount in spirit and enter in,
To places of unearthly loveliness.
There leads a narrow path,—so ran my thought,—
From yonder strait bright postern of the clouds
To the inner region, through steep banks of light
Low-winding, clothed in beauty as of gold
Molten to luminous mist. Yet not of gold
Alone, but myriad-coloured is the light;
For when the climbing pathway serpentine,
Turning at last its topmost angle, gains
A height of outlook,—lovelier than all thought
Lie, forward-glistening with a thousand hues,
The deep rich valleys of the unknown land,
Far-widening to the plain's immensity.
And over all a liquid radiance hangs,
Like to the softness of a summer moon;
It melts the edges of the leaves, and steeps
The outlines of the copses dreamily,
And swims above the hollows and the glens,
And mellows every field and flowery knoll
With shadows clear that are but deeper light.
Far on, within the land's mid-bosom, sleep

The silvery waters, and the little brooks
Shine here and there, and many a brimming curve
Of the broad river is bright between the hills.
But far horizonward, the sight grows faint
For glory of the distant mountain-peaks;
Piled range on range, from misty nothingness,
Through zones of purple gloom, and glimmering
    crags,
Up to the topmost spires of dazzling snow,
Smitten aslant by rainbow-shafted gleams,
And with their white uplifted glistering points
Piercing a purer heaven above the heavens,
The sapphire deeps, translucent, limitless.
And near me on the shelving meadow-slopes
Are groups of bright-haired children, ivory-
    limbed,
Moving with joy among the flowers,—' Nay,
    cease,'
Said a sad inward voice, that brought me back
To the chill evening, and the barren down,
And the blank sky; for, when I looked, the rift
Was closed, and wan November lord of all.
'Dream not. The gate of cloudland only leads
To cloudland; though for many a lustrous league

The upper surface stretches, beautiful,
A broken billowy waste of vapour, rich
With tides of sunset gold.   Else is there nought.'
Then I, like one who heavy-hearted views
A shattered thing of beauty, slowly thought
And spake, 'A heavenly vision profitless,
Untrue, the striving of a man's own thought
For that he would were real, makes him but feel
The cruel bounds that wall his impotence.
Better to brook a rayless world, a void
Accepted.   Is there then no hope for dreams?'
And lifting saddened eyelids I beheld
On the hard ground the gray breath of the east
Driving the helpless skeleton of a leaf.
Then on my spirit fell a weariness :
For though the soft bright vision lingered yet
Of the upper land, I knew the inward voice
Spake truly, that the cloud was only cloud.
Yet still, as loth to deem the open door
An idle fancy, and no further worth
Than for a moment's pleasing, grieved at heart
I wandered up and down the ways of thought
For some more perfect insight ; while the wind
Sang in the naked branches scornfully,

And made through all the landscape's emptiness
Keen inquisition, hunting even the dust
From every crack and crevice of the plain.
Last, something from the inner silence broke :—
'Take heart ! thy dream of beauty was not vain.
For though the world is beautiful, there lives
In every loveliness a haunting trace
Of something still more lovely, not of earth.
Yet no man alway can behold it. Rich
Are they who see it oft, and he that sees
Draws strength as from a draught of heavenly
    wine,
Whose clusters in a starry vineyard grew,
And in the rainbow-tinted starbeam-glows
Hung mellowing, till the ripe star-season brought
The crystal-flooding vintage. All thy life,
Upon its heavenward side, is but a thing
Of glimpses, and of glimmerings, and of doors
Opened and shut again, with outborne sound
Of voices silver-tongued. Wherefore take heart ;
For though the gate of cloudland only leads
To cloudland, yet that other which thou sawest
Within, had spiritual truth ; a glimpse
Of higher things which are in higher worlds.

Before the eyes of men there hangs a veil,
Hiding those higher unknown things, whereto
The deepest tides of soul set evermore.
Some know not of the veil, and walk content
With the scant portion underfoot ; and some
Know, sorrowful, the veil, but long in vain
For opening ; watch thou, for to happier eyes
Come the bright rifts, and many a sight and sound
Is bursting with the inpent divinity.'

IDYL III

BUTTERCUP TIME

THERE is a time in England, the year's crown
If the gold makes the crown, for gold it wears
More sheeny than the yellow harvest-field,
And brighter burnished than the dying leaf.
   Then fills each meadow with a golden flood,
Soft-swimming in between its hoary dykes
The may-bloom hedgerows, islanding the trees,
And many a brake the home of hidden song,
With windings, and long levels, and bright arms,
Till every little ridge is overborne
Of gold waves breaking, and from end to end
Afloat with gold, the many-meadowed vale
Streams a long glitter to its dreamy verge,
Where, like a gentle cliff, the wood upsprings
Clothing the hills with green of summer's youth.
And all the bright drops of the sea are flowers,
Innumerable golden chalices,

Poised every one on slender sap-fed green,
That chains it to its place, yet hinders not
Stir of vibration to the tenderest thrill
Of the young summer's breath. The buttercups
Live in the fire they kindle, and the gold,
Even while its long lines slumber mistily,
Has movement.
     Of all seasons that to me
Most joyful seems in coming of the gold,
Saddest departing; when the cuckoo's flute
Falters as if in dread of empty fields,
And stammers toward his silence; when the tint
Of the full-vestured woodland sobers down,
As if the ecstasy of newborn leaves
Had left it weary; and the bright young grass
Waves mellower underneath its ripening spears.
With silent increase wax the years and wane,
And every month has beauty; but the gold
Comes with the prime,—warm earth and happy
  skies,
Rich odour, painted petal, wingèd song
Meeting the sun, and in all things that live
The strong full-veined upshooting of the life.
And when the valley-tide of golden cups

Floats at the flood, then stands the mounting year
Upon the topmost step of youth, and drinks
The wine of won perfection.

                          So to me,
On the spread lustre feasting thoughtful eyes,
In radiant silence of the summer fields,
Out of the many-meadowed vale there comes
A glimpse of something more than beautiful,
That wraps the soul in easeful warmth; a dream
Of pure perfection wreathed in thornless rose;
A sense unutterable of the glow of life,
Of happiness inborn, which the world's pain
Crushes not out; an instinct sure and deep
Of the joy-giving Power that somewhere sits
Pouring untired on thankless littleness
The streams of ever-welling glory-vials.

  Yet is the old world-haunting pain at hand.
Behind the circled hills the strife of men
Reels fever-flushed, though here unheard; and I
Who drink this dreamy golden opiate,
Am part thereof, thence came and thither go.
Nay, yonder gray and peaceful-glimpsing thatch
Between the elms,—is all thereunder peace?
The green roof-moss that twinkles to the sun

Might cover cruel deeds and smile as bright.
Girdle the globe with fancy's gossamer
Each way from hence,—will any thread return
Untouched of pain ? The brake, the hedge, the grass
Hold war; through conflict slides the silver brook;
My very feet tread battles, and my lips
Draw in the rout of many a tiny host,
Victor with vanquished ; through the range of all,
Life feeds on life, and being climbs to being
O'er piles of crushed existence. Pale with doubt
Grows pleasure musing on life's bitter-sweet.
   But o'er the earth-face here, so passion-marred,
Nigh to the pain, nay rooted in the strife,
Broods this warm golden dream of buttercups,
With such deep power of soothing to the soul,
Such sun-fed atmosphere of strength and youth,
That even in gazing dazzled doubt falls blind,
And hope comes from the hidden heart of things
Upbursting like a pure exhaustless well.

If strife is, summer is ! behold the flowers,
A shoal of starry kisses by love's lips
Imprinted on the earth's pain-furrowed brow.
Who suffers loved, less suffers. Hold the hope !
As one that stood upon a mountain-ledge,
Watching the far-off battle in the plain,
Till some bright-wandering length of morning cloud
Stole up between, and left the lonely crags,
The white peak's holy silence, and the blue,
Might lift his heart and say, 'This sunny peace,
This temple-stillness of the solemn heights,
Is of the things that last, but yonder fray
That reddens and that shrieks behind the cloud,
Will pass forever, with its senseless hate
And them that felt and wrought it; other men
Will come, by wisdom strong and brotherhood,
To till and sow and reap the trampled fields
With golden plenty ; and the stainless peak,
Clothed with the evening like a sacred thought,
Will speak to them of God.' So I who muse
On all creation's battle, men and things,

While round me rich the many-meadowed
    vale
Glows myriad-petalled, feel within my soul
The surging deep of joy unconquerable,
Prophetic of its own eternity.
For there are faculties unnamed, and powers
Unregistered of all philosophy,
And by keen-scenting science yet untracked;
Threads intertwined in tangled consciousness,'
That serve not the rough uses of the world,
Dormant, unprized; but whoso follows them
May find in that the lips call beautiful,
An instinct drawing him to that which is,
Beyond the sense and thought of present
    man;
Not seeing God in things, but through things
    God,
A record and a sign for his own hour,
That borrows not from language of the dead
A time-worn evidence, but builds anew
On sight and insight. So to me is given,
Through musing vision of the valley-gold,
The glimpse of joy whose far-off heritage
Is conquest over slowly-fading pain.

So, when to doubt life seems a shadow-land,
Where the blind battle through the twilight moves,
Love's symbol for hope's eyes, God sets the flowers,
A gleam of mystic writing on the world.

IDYL IV

Kin to the clearness of the central blue
Whereto he winging sang, the skylark's song,
Above the April slopes of wooded knolls,
Above the church yews and the orchard sprays,
And elm-thronged meadows rolling to the sea,
Rose like a summer star, and spread abroad
Like a wide water, and fell back to earth
A silver rain. Ear-captive, motionless,
Blind to the budded beauties of the spring,
I heard, and hearing felt the whole world song.
But while I lived in music, as there comes
On sunny fields the shadow of a cloud,
So sudden on the radiant treble stole
A bell-note deep, whose mellower resonance
Came rich, like memories of the autumn woods,
And toned with autumn sadness. Where the surge
Of budding boughs ringed one dark isle, it spake,

From the old tower amid the older yews.
Pauseless above in airy heights the lark
Sang on ; so made the twain strange harmony,
The wrought bronze heavenward calling close to earth
The wild bird vocal half-way up to heaven.
   The bell came toned with sadness, yet the sound
Touched as with human life the sense too high,
When rushing, rushing, like a mountain stream,
The skylark's passion filled the world. Such joy
Lives but in moments, and the soul's foretaste
Of what it may be, will be, is not now,
Feels sudden earth. Not on one rapture's height,—
So ran thought woven with the bird and bell—
Nor in one sorrow's depth, albeit from each
Look windows on the great world's mystery,
Grows wisdom ripe. Yon many-wintered yews,
Whose branches darkly tent the mouldering sleep,
Which stand like solemn brethren of the tower,
And scarce more bending to the reckless winds,
With change, to which the dial-hands are swift,
Slow-grown above the slowly gathering dead,—

What bygone glances, unuplifted now,
Have loved them, seen the dawn-gold touch
    their tips
From many a lucid east, and many a night
Their sombre masses shore the lake intense
Whereon the moon sails lonely. Minds of men,
Whose every thought is dead ; a firm-set stone,
A planted sapling grown to wondrous girth,
Or some enduring fabric, here and there .
Attest the nameless hands. Yet o'er them hung
The lark-song, and the gray yew-girdled tower
Stood in their midst, and hourly that rich bell
Tolled their full-pulsing present into past.
Dreamless of end, his world was real to each,
And he the centre. Whither are they borne,
The tides of wasted thought, that evermore
Pass from the sunny zone of consciousness,
Into the chill dark unremembered void ?
How swiftly grows upon the soil of earth,
The thing called 'I,' that sets his tiny ring
About a fragment of the infinite,
Saying 'Within, behold myself; without,
The world,' and there abides, yet is but one
Of random multitudes that come and go,

Like settlers on the commonland of time.
And each, as wrapt in his own fervid dreams,
Lives in that point, whose still unstable place
Shifts like the reflex of a wandering light
On darkness thrown, his 'now'; all else is thought;
Behind, a memory; before, a hope.
And each whose life is something more than sleep
Has moods like that the lark-song made in me,
When the slight confines of the present touch
The everlasting, and the wells of life
Leap stronger from their depths, and on the soul
A bright light glimpses from beyond the world.
The little gust that stirs a bank of flowers,
Makes in the petal's pearly loveliness
A moment's heightened beauty, and is gone.
Are those high moments of the conscious self
Mere gusty beauties of the soul, vain gleams
Athwart the vain? Or sows mortality,
Albeit a blindfold sower, to and fro
Pacing within her narrow field of time,
Sure seed, whose harvest shall upgather all
She was, and all she thought, the useless lost
Alone, the husks well sifted from the grain?

Then were the dead thoughts of forgotten
    minds
But to the undiscerning present dead.
Their best still lives in each, and somewhere
    grows
To self-fulfilment. All the nobler past
Has future; nor is theirs an idle work,
Who commune with its records lovingly.
  By yonder tower lies one, borne lately forth
From scholar-walls within the peopled town,
To rest among the green simplicities,
Whose life, that only touched its blameless prime
And faded, had this scope,—with reverent toil
Made master of what thoughts unperishing
Brake like a dawn among the hills of Greece,
Or swayed the soul of sovereign Italy,
To teach young spirits, whose unfolding flower
Was turning on the world with freshness, these,
The parent-thoughts of Europe. Yet to him
Came doubt perchance, though thrilling with the
    life
Of some bright heart-uplifting vision old
He strove to paint, when oft a troubled sound
Of wheels, fast-speeding by his cloister-wall

Warned of the eager world that clashed without,
Half-blinded with the hunger of the hour.
Since, knowing those he taught must plunge
   therein,
He gave them but the inner spirit's gold,
That scantly wins the outer. Many a spring
May wake the wooded knolls, and touch the elms,
And gird the dark-boughed neighbours of his
   rest
With laughing apple-blossom, ere the crown
Of just arbitrament reward his toil,
By end and issue of full-garnered time.
Yet, when the long day of humanity
Draws on to lustrous sunset,—not for night,
But for some sunrise yet unknown,—shall things
Of thought, and heightened moments of the soul
Outlast the growths of shallow circumstance,
And gather toward fulfilment. Then shall he,
As one that knew, and one that helped to know,
Find recompense.   For still the inward life
Runs on through turbid currents of the world,
Now faint, now waxing stronger, watched of
   God;

And they whose vision holds the upper blue,
Shall fare, albeit with weary lengths between,
From lark-song unto lark-song, till the bell
Toll from the shadow-gates, where one by one
Pass out the several selves to fuller light.

IDYL V

THE SNOWCLOUDS

Slowly up from the east, on the breast of the moving wind,
Dazzling white in the morning light, the foremost snowcloud swept;
   Its mighty train, out-stretching a hundred leagues behind,
Floated and flew in the gulfs of blue, and the sun on its forehead slept.

   Slowly onward it sailed, like an icy mountain-chain,
Severed of old when the sphere-storm rolled, and the sphere-flash smote the steep,
   And the adamant anchors of rock brake loose from the solid plain,
Severed and hurled from a ruined world, and launched on the endless deep.

Like a mountain-chain adrift, the column of snowclouds came;
But its rounded swells and shadowy dells and melting heights were soft,
Changing and curling ever, like smoke that curls from a flame,
When a wild fire flies, and a forest dies, and its thick breath gathers aloft.

Softer than hills, they seemed like a shoal of Titans to glide,
Goddesses fair through seas of the air slow-voyaging hand-in-hand,
With an endless snowy gleam of shoulder and bosom and side,
To some sea-verge where the saffron surge breaks warm on a white star-strand.

Over the sun-steeped blue they passed till they covered the sun,
Covered the blue, and a great gloom grew, and a change on the face of things,

For each way out of the clouds seemed dark-flung pinions to run
Through the heavens wide in an eddying tide ever duskier, wings upon wings.

The strong wind stopped as in awe, and the dark-faced heavens were dumb,
Mute was the hill, and the valley still, and silence over the seas,
Silence, as if upon nature a speechless sorrow were come;
Heard in the hush was the far stream's rush, and a scarce-felt shiver of trees.

Then out of the silence, tears, till between the earth and the skies
The air grew light with the flying white, white tears from a darkness deep,
Tears that feather-like fell without sound of sobbing or sighs,
And fallen lay still in the hollows chill or clung to the sunless steep.

Then after the weeping, smiles, and a sweet
    sun-gleam on the snow,
Diamonds a-light in the field's wide white, and
    gold on the failing flake,
Till the tears had end, and in heaven the clear
    blue laughed, and below,
The grass-point was risen o'er its melting prison,
    and the bare twig glanced in the brake.

Then thought I who had watched the shapes
    of the great cloud-host
Gather and pass on the sky and the grass till
    they faded out of my sight,
Lo, thus do the great generations of men roll
    by to be lost,
Sunk in the glooms of forgotten tombs and the
    silence of endless night.

Suddenly out of the deep, and the dark that
    no man knows,
Eddying crowds, more thick than the clouds,
    they come and they cover the earth,

Bright for a while in their strength, then lost at last as the snows,
Passing away like a dying day that sets on the land of its birth.

Yea, and weeping is theirs, for if gaudy of outward hue,
The garment of life they weave in the strife of their few and fervent years
Glows like a summer garden with scarlet and purple and blue,
Under the bright is the wan and the white, and the secret channel of tears.

The tears of men are warm, but grief far down in the heart
Chills life's flood at the founts of the blood and makes it cold as the snow,
And lips may smile with the smile of the stone that is shapen of art,
Ash of the fire and dust of desire in the frozen soul below.

Yet were they beautiful tears that the great soft snowclouds wept,
Caught by the sun ere the storm was done, and melting in crystal and gold;
And sweet gleams lighted the grief of the men that have long since slept,
Rainbow dyes on the rain of the eyes that melted with sorrows of old.

For tears are beloved of God, and a beauty there is of grief,
Tints on the foam as the tide shifts home, a beauty of that which will die;
And not the sunbeam alone, but the raindrop blesses the leaf,
Blinding showers, then gold on the flowers, from this world's April sky.

Courage! the beauty that glimpses in tears is a beauty of hope.
Life in the light, then the grave and the night, and it seems but little we know;

The world's way wearily winds at the foot of a cloud-crowned slope,
But the top cloud's gloom has a tender bloom like the burst of a rosy glow.

And never in vain, perchance, has a single mourner wept;
Fallen snows live though they vanish, and give green life to the faded sod;
Dead men's griefs are forgotten on earth, yet sure there is kept
Room for the tears of a million years in the infinite heart of God.

IDYL VI

A MYSTERY OF MORNING

The sun is in the dew;
One heaven of snowy stars with golden eyes,
The daisy-sward all shining lies,
And tiny jets of gold-dust rise
Where the wild bee flew;
Though o'er the lowland dim
The idle mists yet swim,
On this high down that stands apart
The light is full, and light my spirit fills,
As deep into my heart
Passes the beauty of the morning hills.

Yet seems it, while I gaze,
Not of this morn the loveliness alone,
But blent with some soft undertone
Of dreamy beauty, not its own,
From the far-off days;

The glisten and the glow
Some sweeter memories know
Of clear dawns faded from the earth,
Or else some hope of sunbeams yet unborn :
When will their light have birth ?
When wilt thou break, O bright ideal morn ?

O surely not for nought
Comes that strange gleam that haunts all lovely
    things,
That undersong the spirit sings,
When through the eye rich beauty wings
To the deeps of thought !
Lo, I who fain would rest
Content with nature's best,
Which all my life I chiefly love,
Rest not, but feel, when nature's best I see,
Dark cravings in me move,
For something past and lost, or yet to be.

Holds then my heart to-day
A bygone bliss, of some bright moment born,
Some far-off mother's marriage-morn,
With may-bloom on the sunny thorn

In an old-world May?
Can in the memory rise
Delights of other eyes?
Is this strange note that haunts my mood,
Remembered pleasure, heirloom of the race,
Still throbbing in my blood,
As when it flushed my dead forefather's face?

Strange echoes too, more near,
Call me, from childhood's half-remembered hours,
Mixed with the sweet faint scent of flowers,
With lights half-caught from lilac bowers,
Or a still pool clear;
The conscious brain no trace
Keeps of their time or place,
Save when the under-self awakes,
That lies, as hidden waters, deep below,
And silent record makes.
Creeps aught of these athwart the morning glow?

From childhood, or before,
Sound on, ye echoes sweet, and thrill my soul!
I count you sweet, but not the whole.
That vague unrest has further goal,

For it makes thought soar
Far up, beyond the span
Of earth, and mortal man,
Where, with its time-robe all outworn,
My new-winged spirit strong shall, after night,
See glories of the morn
Break the gold clouds, on some eternal height.

IDYL VII

SHORE THOUGHTS

I

Betwixt the wood and the sea
  Is a meditative place;
For a song goes out from the tree
  To the water's upturned face,
And the wave that wanders free
  Sings back from its rocky base.

II

Wood-song, when the leaves are young, and the mild wind-whispers creep,
Wave-song, when the great sea dreams, and the ripples are smiles in his sleep,
Two songs blended in one, through the sun-thrilled ether of spring,
From the bare sea's border of flowers, and the flowery earth's foam-ring;

Two songs blended and sad, when the leaves are a yellow rain,
And the ripples are lost in the dark of the wind-lashed mountainous main,
Wave-wail, when the breakers roar, and the sea-bird shrieks in his flight,
Wood-moan, when the long long wind lays siege to the branch all night.

III

Two songs, sympathy-bound,
    Of two worlds side by side,
Wood-world fixed to its ground,
    Wave-world wandering wide,
With an undersong profound
    From the deep that both worlds hide.

IV

Wood-world, where the vigour of earth mounts up through fibre and cell,
Till the slow-wrought miracle stands, firm-rooted and fashioned well,

The tall tree gentle and strong, brow-bound in the glory of leaves,
A hero in dawn's wind-battle, a spirit in solemn eves.
Wood-world, temple of trees, dark-pillared, odorous-aisled,
Marvellous, melody-haunted, adorable, shadowy, wild,
Where rises the chaos of columns, o'er-marbled with sunbeam-glows,
Baseless from mists of the bracken; where cloistered blossoms repose
In windless solemn arcades; where many a mid-wood niche
Lies roofed like a shadow-shrine from the sun in a gloom so rich,
That the gnats seem tiny stars when their dance whirls by it at noon,
And the great white butterfly fares through the dusk like a crumpled moon.

V

Wave-world, restless of face, deep-hearted; mirror of skies;
Rocked on the broad and wheel-swift bosom of earth as she flies,
And sucking, in many a soft-curved bay, the sweets of the land,
Where the sundering river-mouth pours, through the bar of boulder and sand,
The tremulous treasure of rills, and the freshness of reedy wells,
And the crystal that bubbled cold out of moonbeam-smitten fells.
Wave-world, out of the wastes of whose wandering wilderness
The shoreward-shouldering long foam-helmeted legions press
To the margin-touch, then back to the murmuring gardens gray,
Where the breeze, like a lone day-lily, grows balmy and fades away,

Where the great space shudders and shrieks to the might of the unknown storm,
And the vaporous ranges of gold at the limit of evening form,
And the starry walls of the night, with the stardome canopied o'er,
Leap sheer from the ebon expanse of the silvery-flashing floor.

VI

Deep of the deep, wherefrom, like a couple of neighbour flowers,
Wave-world blossoms in foam, and wood-world opens its bowers,
Sister-worlds to the eye, but to thought on her wonder-wings,
Just two flowers in the measureless meadow of lovely things.
Deep whence beauty on beauty upquivering, birth upon birth,
Build for ever the beauty of sea and the beauty of earth,

Where the thronging shapes come up from the void, like the coming of mist,
Where the gulfs are a dim forever of infinite amethyst,
And the inner nothingness blooms into outlines speakingly fair,
Colours that sing in the leaf, and sounds that silver the air,
And marvels of motion and breath, soul-tenanted, daintily wrought,
Rare cups for the rubied brimming of life and love and thought.
Deep, the despair of the eye and the ear, to the musing mind
In quiet solitudes known, like the lapse of a noiseless wind,
In the mood that listens and leans and loves, and can almost hear
The roving breeze of beginning astir in the ether clear,
And the rustle of new-winged joys with their primal dawn-dews pearled,
And the gush of the atom-streams from the hidden wells of the world.

VII

Wild song, for ear too deep,
   Which the beautiful silence sings,
Which comes like a music in sleep
   To my heart from the heart of things,
While the ripple-shimmers upcreep
   To the leaf's green quiverings;
World-song, filling the place
   Where the woodland shadows the sea,
With the voice of the infinite space
   And the voices of wave and of tree,
Till the music of nature's face
   Makes music of mind in me.

VIII

Thought-world, song of the mind, which she
   chants in her lonely seat,
Poised in the azure abyss, where the stranger
   world-winds meet,

And o'er it the white clouds float, that change with the changing day
Rift and vista and breach, yet roll not ever away;
Chants from her centre of life, where she, to herself unknown,
Woke like a startled child that wakes in a crowd alone;
Woke and wondered and sang, and painted a world in her song,
Painted her dream of things, and her vision of right and wrong,
Fashioned fragment-wise with odour and sound and hue
Her gleam-built fabric of thought, and trusted her thought was true.
And somewhere in all her songs is the sound of a shadowy shore,
Where tides of the great unknown make music for evermore
On narrow sands of the known, and voices over the bar
Quiver with clear-winged hope, like a tremulous lucid star.

For world is mated to world, as the wood looks over the sea;
And when thought reaches the marge of the things that seem to be,
And sings of the sister-world she craves with a pure desire,
The soul of her melody burns like the flame of a silver fire.

IX

To stand where the time-waves roll,
    For the infinite truth to long,
One part in the mighty whole,
    Immortal, prescient, strong,
This is the song of my soul,
    And is it only a song?

LYRICAL PIECES

D

LYRICAL PIECES

ROSE BIRTH

WHITE wild-rose bud, half awake,
  Out of thy sunny cradle peer,
In swaying green above the brake,
And from thine opening eyelid shake
  The dewdrop tear.

Thy little life unfolds to bliss,
  Thy first friend is the morning sun,
What birth could be more fair than this?
The breezes bring thee thy first kiss,
  Thou tender one.

Awake, spread out thy lids of pearl,
  And let the willing sunbeam's light
Make sparkles on the golden whorl
Within; no more thy petals furl
  Until to-night.

The bee will, as he hies along,
    Dip down to touch thee on the face;
Lighthearted birds the whole day long
Will make the soft air sweet with song
    About thy place.

Above thee, wide-eyed innocent,
    All day the balmy brooding blue
Will hang, and when the light is spent,
The evening breezes gathering scent
    For thine will sue.

Live through to-day, while gently creep
    The dial-hands from hour to hour,
Thy life that never needs to weep;
Then fold thee to thy starlight sleep,
    Thou happy flower

THE ELM

On the frozen meadow-slope,
  The elm, a frozen giant, stands,
Like a tomb of summer's hope
  Towering o'er the mournful lands.

When the eastwind cuts at noon,
  Patient of its bitter breath,
Patient, when the blinded moon
  Sinks in rushing sleet to death;

Dumb, unless the nightbird wail,
  Shivering, from its branches bare,
Or the fierce and flying gale
  Blow an icy trumpet there.

Yet there wakes an April dawn,
  When the sunbeam, opening slow
On the green and living lawn,
  Finds its monarch elm aglow.

From the trembling topmost sprays
    Downward through the mighty pile,
To the vast and knotted base,
    Deepening spreads a giant smile.

Myriads shining in the sun
    Burst the little leaf-buds new,
Burst and laugh, and every one
    Bears its own bright pearl of dew.

Soon the full mid-summer pride
    Of the leafage shall be stirred
By mid-summer winds, and hide
    While he sings, the happy bird.

Gaze and hope, O man of grief,
    In thy winter of despair!
Joy will break, as breaks the leaf,
    From the frozen heart of care.

THE SCOTCH FIR

Close to the cloven vapour-streams
That bar the blue with pearly strips,
A dusky cloud, the treetop dreams;
And while, above, it swims and towers,
Its base the rosy column dips
In tumbling seas of grass and flowers.

A charm there is, that baffles words,
About its lifted head, the place
Of sunbeams and of singing-birds;
A plot of earthly green, that yet
To heavenward seems a little space
Caught up, and on a pillar set.

It turns a sad eye bright, to view
The dark-green masses poise and shake
Their clustered needles in the blue;

To see the sunshaft, striking them,
A thousand glints and glimmers make;
And O the blush upon the stem!

Such stems, dividing distance, lend
The land romance that has no name;
Edge sleeping plains with colour, send
Warm pink athwart the shadowy grays,
Set richly the dim hills, and frame
With rosy bars the light-blue haze.

In winter when the world is bare,
Let ne'er so faint a ray of sun
Touch, tremulous in the misty air,
The trunk, and catch the sea-green spines,—
Across wan fields and fallows dun
A painted gleam the fir-tree shines.

But most of all the charm I own,
When after frosty close of day,
Through orange vapours, paler grown,
Peers the first diamond eye of even
Close o'er the tree,—that seems to say
'Look up, and climb by me to heaven.'

ARBOR PONTICA

With richest clusters, o'er its own
Dark depths of leafage starlike sown,
   The purple-throated rhododendron
     Blooms in the glade alone.

No leaf, nor other flower is there,
Nor sward; the one growth everywhere,
   On sides, and level midst, and summit,
     Cast as a mantle fair.

One softly-woven harmony,
The rhododendrons and the sky;
   A lonely isle in nature's ocean,
     Fit for a lonely eye.

Here might one dream content, and doubt
The worth of the broad world without,
   Watching the still, consummate beauty
     Compass the glen about;

Or on forgetful forehead feel
The Anatolian breezes steal,—
   So lost the belt of English woodland
     Seems, which the banks conceal.

For not seed-laden winds, but men
Wooed the dark-foliaged alien
   From thick-grown coppice-haunts of Pontus,
     Bride for an English glen.

Nor native grace is here alone;
The sweetness has a distant tone,
   A fragrancy of far remembrance,
     Over the wide waves blown:

Like banished love that burneth long;
Or captive genius shining strong;
   Or Israel's harp by old Euphrates,
     Tuned to a deathless song.

A CHARACTER

A SETTLED quiet, void of change,
A cloud that moves not from her face,
Is hers, through all her daily range
Of household work from place to place;
She works as in a dream, and yet
No little task does she forget.

Not with clear light, but sadly glow
The deep dark lustres of her eyes,
The reflex of some inward woe;
She looks as if no flush could rise
Through the fixed whiteness of her cheeks,
And yet she brightens when she speaks.

If some light chance should call a smile
About her tender lips to play,
It lingers not, but just awhile
It lives, as on a changeful day
In gleamy gardens comes and goes
The sun upon a snow-white rose.

She works; within her quiet soul
She sees one sight and only one,—
Green waves for ever toss and roll
About a ship, that still doth run,
Bearing through calms and stormy breeze
Her life's one light across the seas.

Yet for herself she never weeps;
For griefs of others, great or small,
Her pitying heart and tears she keeps;
She knows that God is over all.
So flowers, by plucking half undone,
Still try to smile, and face the sun.

A POTENT MEMORY

BLUE eyes, that turned
　As sped the wheels away,
Blue eyes, that burned
　And burn my soul alway,

Come when I wake
　To my long day forlorn;
My daylight make,
　Before the eyes of morn.

When noon shines glad,
　Its crown of gladness be;
If eve wax sad,
　Look through her gloom at me.

Look up from flowers,
　Be bright in driving rain,
Look from gray towers,
　And golden fields of grain;

To all I see,
   Let your twin wells of blue
Like jewels be,
   Set foremost in the view;

Magicians twain,
   To wake my heart to song,
To conquer pain,
   And stay my hands from wrong.

But when still night
   Breaks off the world's control,
Make loveliest light
   In silence of my soul.

ROUGH WINDS AT NIGHT

I HEARD them wailing, wailing,
    Above the midnight town,
I heard them rushing, roaring,
    Over the long bare down;
With a whistle through the shivering bent,
    A moan in the waving pine,
Away to the broad dark main they went,
    To madden the tossing brine.

Why fare ye on, ye mad winds,
    Upon such furious wings,
Where floats the farthest sea-weed,
    And the last seabird sings,
Beyond the last cloud's gloomy bars,
    Rimmed with the moonbeam bright,
Far forward, under silent stars,
    Into the great dim night?

O somewhere, wildly rushing,
    Your swift breath, upward borne
Against an eastern hilltop,
    Will strike into the morn,
And meet in shadowy belts of palm
    That sparkle with the dew,
The newborn sunshine golden-calm,
    Climbing the quiet blue !

And there your mænad music
    That shrieked along the wave,
Hushed by the bright-eyed morning,
    Shall cease at last to rave ;
As some hard man that stormed and strove
    In moody anger wild,
Met by a sudden glance of love,
    Grows gentle as a child.

There shall your breath, grown gentle,
    The sunny leaves among,
Just stir the small bird's feathers,
    That sings his matin song ;

And she that doth her pitcher bear
  Down to the dipping-place,
Shall feel you soft about her hair,
  And fresh against her face.

A GARDEN

There is a lovely lawn, that rests
Upon the shoulder of a steep;
About it rise the hilly crests,
Yet with the vale it seems to keep
Communion too, as if its love
Went half below and half above.

The far blue mountains on the right
Mix with the clouds, but leftward seen
The forest flings from height to height
Its sunny-glinting mantle green,
And where its lowest shadow sleeps,
By curving banks the river creeps.

In front, the cedars half retire,
And show, beneath a sheltering ridge,

A little town, with one tall spire,
That stretches toward a dusky bridge,
Where under three dark arches gleam
The silver eddies of the stream.

And pacing on that lawn at eve,
I hear a hundred voices call,
From forests that the sunbeams leave,
And from the purpling mountain-wall,
And from the water, glimmering down
Through twilight shadows to the town.

O voices sweet, I do you wrong;
With such a spell my heart is drawn
From you, to one who lingers long
In yonder house beside the lawn :
With straining ear, and heart astir,
I watch the garden-door for her.

A CITY SIGH

THE idle breeze at evening
That roameth ever and ever away,
Through a land of shadows, quiet and gray,
    Ever, by hill and by hollow,
    Faring on to the dreamy west,
    To far-off misty meadows of rest,—
      Had I but wings to follow,
      At waning of weary day!
      Had I but wings to follow,
For day lies heavy over the town,
And, dropped through still air slowly down,
    Like darts from a tired Apollo,
    Upon the redhot miles of brick
    The stagnant sunbeams swelter thick;
      And ever emptier seems,
To men who toil in house or street,
The labour of brain and hands and feet,
A noisy nothing in noontide heat,
      A wrangle of dying dreams,

That wear the heart and dim the sight;
And as they toil in lessening light,
Choked with the city's breath like blight,
The day burns out to smouldering night.
    But, far away,
  The idle breeze, the light breeze
Is up and roaming at eventide,
Stirring the reeds at the riverside,
  Skimming the pool like a swallow,
Catching a bar from the song of the rill,
To drop in the ear of the drowsy hill,
  And dipping down to the hollow,
Where darkening ferns hang, dewy and deep,
And still, tall spires of foxglove sleep,
  And twilight mysteries creep;
O'er lonely fields that the willows skirt,
By farms and hamlets orchard-girt,
And pastures where the cattle rest,
And long dales dimly winding west,
A wayward air, for ever astray,
Through a land of shadows, quiet and gray,
  Had I but wings to follow,
  At waning of weary day!

BY A GRAVE

Lilies in the valley,
   Harebells on the hill,
And in the meadow buttercups,
   And wild-rose by the rill;
But only daisies in the turf,
   Where my love lies still.

Overhead the heaven,
   Where the skylarks soar,
And round about, the waving boughs
   As sunny as before;
But the sun that lit this life for me
   Is set for evermore.

DISTANCE

I

LIKE one, who, gazing under lifted hand
Beyond the salt breadth of an ocean-strait,
Views a fair unknown coast, disconsolate,
And loves the distant land;
So my eyes watch, to wistful steps denied,
The purple-dented misty mountain-mass,
To whose gray feet, far off, the lowland-tide
Rolls her dim woods and desolate morass;
Dreaming of cool and cataract-voiced ravines
Too far for sight; and many a heavenward lawn,
Light's forefront at the dawn;
And each noon-shadowing rock that downward
    leans;
And all the hamlet-nursing valley-folds,
With peasant peace and low-eaved quiet filled,
When streaks of sunset gild
What hanging red the laden orchard holds.

II

So too, when o'er the lustrous dreamy deeps,
Shoreless, star-islanded, a moving net
Stranded of cloud, by fisher night-winds set,
With mesh inconstant creeps,
While, haloed on its shifting pearl, the moon
Burns bronze, and radiant quietude descends
Even to the incensed blossom-sleep of June
That compasses my feet; a hunger blends
With joy of night's high loveliness. The cloud
Calls me; the bright moon beckons; and the wind
Sighs, leaving me behind;
The very gleams are voices, and grow loud;
And far beyond the film-bar's drift, the spheres,
Where isled in deep lagoons, they glimmer through
The fleecy-broidered blue,
Sound out a silver clarion in my ears.

III

Yet, could I by desiring melt the chains
Of fleshly life's condition, and take wing
To the utmost jewel of the utmost ring
Earth-centred sight attains,

That seems a spark, though far remote it flares
A great orb glory-vestured; even such flight
Would cradle newborn longing. As who dares
By dizzy paths upclimb an isthmus-height,
The gulf's rock-girdle, finds the further side
As great a world of waves; so that high place
Would look on rolling space,
Whereto this whole star-spangled region wide,
Whose multitudinous miles are as the sand,
Is but the gate : where universes vain
Sink like the drops of rain
In yawning fields by timorous thought unspanned.

IV

Out of the virgin deeps forever rise
New siren-songs; and, like thought's nemesis,
The looming of the unbeheld abyss
Round each horizon lies.
From narrow 'now' and 'here,' fast-bound in flowers
Or thorn-beset, the argus-visioned soul
Takes outlook; sees millenniums brief as hours,
A finger's breadth the space from pole to pole,

And either way the ranging infinite
Within the greater and the less grow dim;
And alway, like a hymn,
Upwells the longing for far-off delight.
For life is as a boat that sees no shore;
Yet shall they find the freedom of the land,
And leap upon the strand,
Who now must tend the rudder and the oar.

AT AN OPEN WINDOW

THE stars are awake,
   The flowers asleep;
The odorous airs
   In the night-hush deep,
Through the jasmine-garlanded casement creep.

The silvery shafts
   On the clasped hands shine
Of a kneeling girl,
   And her hair divine,
As she prays in her scented, starlit shrine.

The starlight rains pure;
   Sweet incense is blown;
But the sweet, pure thoughts
   Are winging alone,
Through a star-bloomed firmament, all their own.

WAVING GRASS

When tired thought flags and the life burns low,
    And wearier waxes the world of men,
There is virtue of healing where green things grow,
    And the quiet of fields is a power, then;
But most,—to wander and watch at will
The ripple of grass on a windy hill.

A witchery lives in the swaying stems,
    A riddle of motion, an anodyne
Of voiceless pæans and requiems,
    That waken the heart like a wizard wine;
Yet no man fathoms the spell of the grass,
That flutters and bends when the young winds pass.

Does the trace of the travelled winds beget
　A mind fresh-visioned and burden-free ?
The dream of their fairy footprints, set
　In the surge of the thousand-bladed sea ?
And the pulse of their unspent wings, new-born
In a golden dew at the gates of the morn ?

Is it charm of the grass-stalk, lithe and lush,
　From its downward-dipping gusty swing
Recoiling, at lull of the light wind's rush,
　To its sunward poise, with a pliant spring,
Uprearing straight from the stem-thronged ground
A spear-host, tremulous, blossom-crowned ?

Or is it the ripple-tide, rhythmic, strong,
　Yet changeful as tongues of the flickering fire,
The wave-chant, the sinuous shudder-song
　Of the many-bending, green-robed choir,
A music of motion whose tones are curves,
As its serpentine melody slides and swerves ?

Be it music, freshness, or unseen wind,
  That fancy may name the enchanter's power,
The fugitive mystery lurks behind,
  Like a honey-fount hid in the heart of a flower.
Let the tired eyes drink, and the barren brain!
They search for the secret source in vain.

THE TURNING FROM THE GRAVE

I

Like a last cloud, that fills
    The last blue space,
Ere the rain hides the hills,
    Dimming earth's face,
One moment, sad, supreme,
    Comes at grief's height,
Waking from sorrow's dream
    To sorrow's night.
Bitter, the faint farewell
    Helpless to hear!
Bitter, the slow-swung bell,
    The slow-borne bier!
Yet, to be doing stole
    Part of grief's ill;
The last rite brings the soul
    Bitterer still,

When he whose love and trust
   Lie there below,
Last, from the graveside must
   Turn him to go.

II

To go,—what matter where?
   Homeless is grief.
The field-flowers may be fair,
   Sunlit the leaf;
Pearl-cup and jewel-bell,
   And starry gold;
Birdsong in primrose dell;
   Cloudlet's soft fold;
Painfully beautiful!
   Now grown, to him,
One picture, blurred and dull,
   Distantly dim.

III

He is not of it! No,
   Let the world lie
Fettered in frozen snow,
   While the winds cry,

Where in the iron dell
  Lies the bird dead,
Where the shrill sleet-cloud's swell
  Slings overhead,
Where falls the icy dark
  The flower-graves o'er :—
The change his eye might mark ;
  Grief were not more.
Summer-bloom, winter-gloom
  To him all one ;
One season at the tomb
  Endless begun.

IV

To go,—no matter where !
  Down the dim street ;
Through the smoke-stifled air ;
  Where the stones meet
Over the flower-stript earth,
  Their prison old,
Crushing its blossom-birth
  With lordship cold ;

The thronging crowd to thread,
    Outlived of stones
Whereon to-day they tread;
    The myriad tones
Of the great city-soul,
    Heedless, to hear,
To watch its life-wheels roll,
    Nor feel them near;
Cast with that stranger crowd
    A space, soon fled!
Do they too feel the shroud?
    Have they their dead?

V

Homeward? nay, 'home' no more,
    Only a place,
Where once an opening door
    Showed a bright face!
Where,—was it years ago?
    Nested love smiled;
Winds through the nest-rifts blow
    Chill, now, and wild!

Back to that ghost of home?
  But for life's need,
Better o'er wilds to roam
  Till the feet bleed;
Better one wandering
  Home of unrest,
Till the last shadows bring
  Love repossessed.
Back? to the chamber lone,
  The untrodden stair?
Where for the wonted tone
  Listens the air,
Where from the barren walls
  Memories steal;
There, as night's silence falls,
  The truth to feel?

VI

The truth? ah, vain to wait
  Earthly relief!
The graveside is the gate
  Of lonely grief.

Enter, and face despair !
　　　　Best is home's blank.
　　　Watch the faint traces there
　　　　Where the sun sank !
　　　Duty makes sober light
　　　　Where shadows are :
　　　Homeward ! to truth the night,
　　　　And faith the star.

A SPRING FANCY

THE light May-breeze is gone to sleep,
   And sunny stillness holds the glen,·
In sheets of bluebells lying deep,
    Far from the ways of men.

The mute copse has a listening air;
   As if in deepest hush alone
The faint bell-blossoms rang; a rare
    And hyacinthine tone.

Some silver chimes in all that crowd
   Of sapphire belfries washed with dew
Must sure be falling, low or loud,
    Had I but hearing true!

At daybreak did no dainty peal
   Wake up the drowsy bee? To-night
Will ne'er a fragrant curfew steal
    To shut the glow-worm's light?

Even now, when sleeps without a sound
    The silence of the scented blue,
The perfume from the loaded ground
    So strikes my senses through,

I scarce believe mere odour sweet
    So rich a joy of soul could bring,
Or make in one sensation meet
    All raptures of the spring.

Comes not this sunshine at my heart
    In the still, azure-sheeted dell,
From music, like the tears that start
    At some far wind-borne bell?

Then let me follow fancy's bent,
    And dream this little dream of spring,
That in the wafting of the scent
    I hear the bluebells ring!

FOUR zones in yonder evening sky
Each over other, blended lie.

The first is level amethyst,
Where the sea sleeps in folded mist ; ·

Orange the next, that dreams of red,
With olive cloudlets overspread ;

The third is the void saffron, clear
As April drops that dint the mere ;

Last, glistens in pale phantom-blue
Arcturus faint, like trembling dew.

Printed by BALLANTYNE, HANSON & CO.
Edinburgh & London

www.ingramcontent.com/pod-product-compliance
Lightning Source LLC
Chambersburg PA
CBHW031604110426
42742CB00037B/1098